SIDEWALK FOSSILS

SIDEWALK

 WALKER AND COMPANY · NEW YORK

FOSSILS

text and
photographs by
**Robert Sommer
and
Harriet Becker**

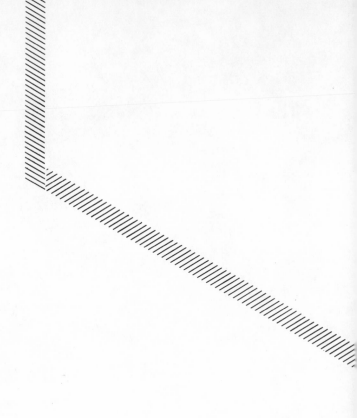

First published in the United States of America in 1976 by the
Walker Publishing Company, Inc.

Published simultaneously in Canada by
Fitzhenry & Whiteside, Limited, Toronto.

Trade ISBN: 0-8027-6228-X
Reinf. ISBN: 0-8027-6233-6

LIBRARY OF CONGRESS CATALOG CARD NUMBER: 75-10056
Printed in the United States of America.

Book design by Robert Bartosiewicz

10 9 8 7 6 5 4 3 2 1

To Sara and Martha

Every day in towns and cities, new sidewalks are being made and old sidewalks are being fixed. Sometimes, when the sidewalk is wet, marks are left by leaves, people, or animals. Leaves fall down on the wet cement. Twigs, seeds, or pine cones get mixed into the cement by mistake. In time they wear away but leave their outline. Dogs and cats walk across the wet cement and leave their footprints. Cement companies may leave their names right on the sidewalk. In this way, many sidewalk fossils are being made every day.

Dinosaur track

Long ago dinosaurs and other animals stepped in soft
wet mud. Sometimes the mud dried and preserved their
footprints for us to see now. When these footprints and
other traces of animal life are very old, scientists call
them fossils. They believe a true fossil has to be more
than ten thousand years old. The tracks and prints you
find in the sidewalk aren't nearly as old as this. This is
why we call them sidewalk fossils instead of real fossils
like dinosaur tracks.

Sidewalk fossils can be found almost everywhere. Start by looking close to your home. A good place to find leaf fossils is on the sidewalk, under a row of trees. In a downtown area there are sometimes old sidewalks that have dates in them and the names of the people who made them. On street corners you may find the name of the street printed in it. Or look for newly laid sidewalks. They are usually lighter in color than old sidewalks and it is easier to pick out the fossils. Any time of day when the light is good can be used for fossil hunting. The main thing is to walk slowly because fossils are hard to find.

Most sidewalks are made of concrete. Concrete is a mixture of cement, sand, broken stone, and water. The mixture has to be stirred together in a cement mixer. Sometimes this is done on a big truck.

Cement mixer

The wet concrete is poured into molds. These
are usually straight boards on both sides of the
walk. The mixture gets stronger and harder
as it dries. If something falls on the wet concrete
it will leave a mark. This is why workmen put
fences around wet sidewalks to keep people
away. Some people were here anyway.
Notice the marks.

When a sidewalk is finished, the maker of the sidewalk sometimes prints his name in the wet concrete.
Sometimes he puts down the date the sidewalk was made.

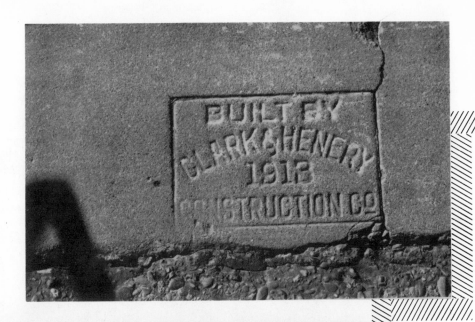

Sixteen could be a house number or
the number of the block.

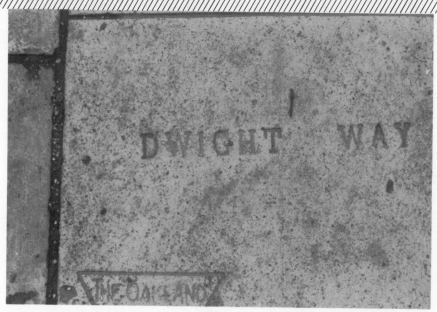

Sometimes the name of the street is printed
into the sidewalk at the ends of the block.

A person made this fossil.   The shoe tells a story.
Look at it closely.
The toe is pointed and
there is a small heel.
It is probably a woman's shoe.

Here are two footprints. Two different
people made the prints because
one is much bigger than the other.
The one on the right is deeper. Did
one person walk on it when the cement
was softer? Or did a heavier person
make the deeper track? Which
do you think it is?

One of the two people who walked
in this cement was barefoot.
Or did the same person take off a shoe
and make another print?

Someone who wore sneakers
or rubber-soled shoes
made these tracks.
The shoes look new.
We can tell that because
the treads are high.

Different sneakers
have different
patterns
on their soles.

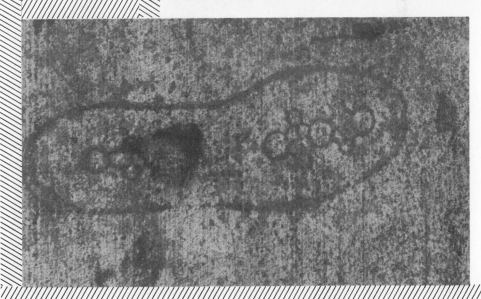

This fossil was not made by just stepping in wet cement. Somebody either slipped or slid on it. Maybe that is what the person wanted to do, but maybe the concrete was very slippery.

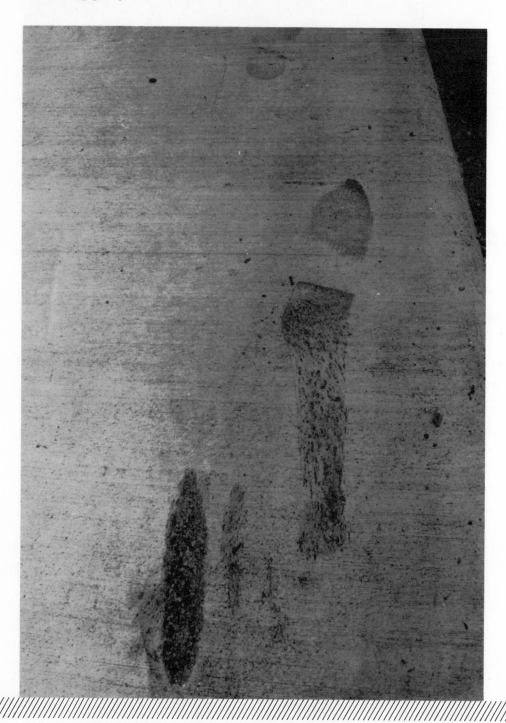

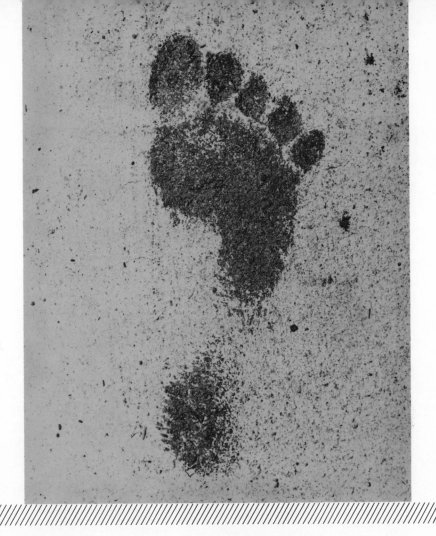

Was this made by someone's right or left foot?

Was this print made by a right or left hand?

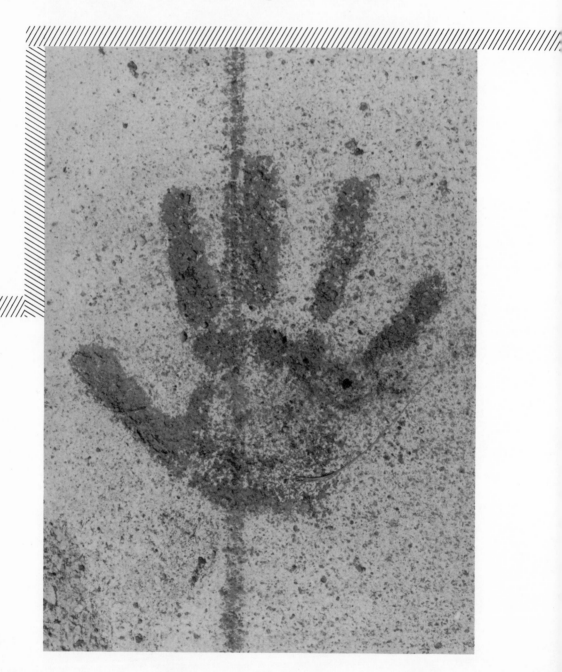

Here are two handprints, a date, and a footprint.
The person who made the footprint is much smaller
than the one who made the handprints.

Do you think a horse made this print or
did someone put a horeshoe down on the sidewalk?

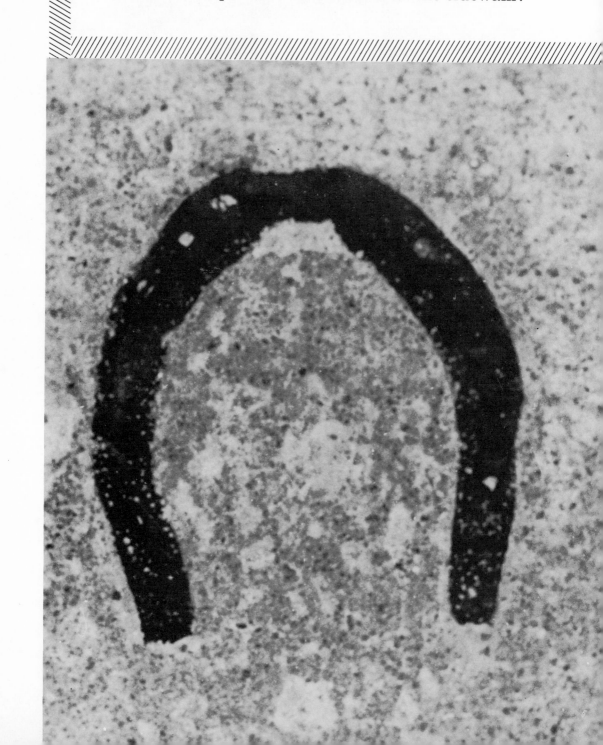

There are more dog prints than cat prints in
sidewalks because most sidewalks are laid
during the day when dogs are outside.
Cats usually wait until dark before
they walk around the neighborhood.
Also, cats do not like wet concrete.

But this is a cat print.
You can tell because no claws show.

Some people made drawings in the wet concrete.

Is this someone's pet goldfish or
is it another kind of fish?

This cat must
be a pet too.

What do you think this is—Donald Duck or
a pet parakeet?

The jack-o'-lantern
makes you think
of Halloween.

Two bicycles passed by.
One might have had the heavier load.
Or maybe the cement dried more before
the left one made its track.

Both of these flying toys must have
landed
in the
wet
concrete.

Some street fossils
are of people's names
written in the
sidewalk.
Estella and Rudi
wrote their names here.
They must have had
a long stick
to reach over that far
without leaving
footprints.

And here we see that M loves Y.

You may be able to tell something about the kind of people who live in a neighborhood by the language you find written on the sidewalk.

This looks as though someone signed his or her name in Chinese in 1939. Perhaps a lot of Chinese people lived in the neighborhood. But maybe a Chinese man or woman just passed by in a neighborhood where no Chinese people lived. It's hard to tell by one street fossil.

When the shadow of the building
falls on this sidewalk clock,
it tells you the time of day.

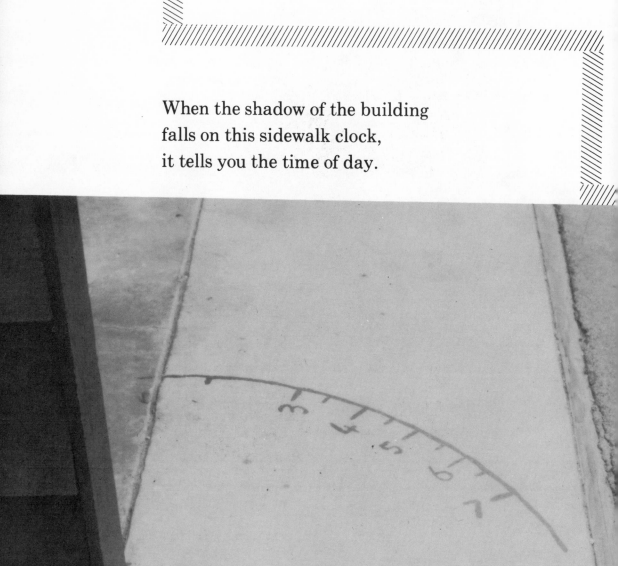

Leaves are the most common street fossils.
Which one of these is the real leaf?

Did the small leaf fall on the wet concrete
before or after the large leaf?

Maple

Hackberry

These leaves were mixed in with the cement.
It was probably late summer or autumn
when leaves fall from the trees.
You can tell what kind of leaves they are
by the shape.

Poplar

Oak

Here are some mystery fossils.
Can you figure out what they are?

This fossil is from a tree.

What kind of wrapper does this look like?

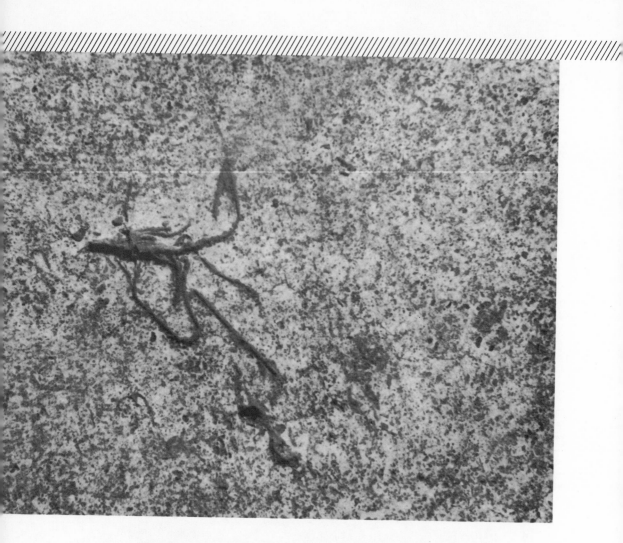

Could this be a string from a package?

What animal tried out the wet cement?

Is this a shell or a thumbprint?

If you want to copy a sidewalk fossil,
                        make a rubbing.

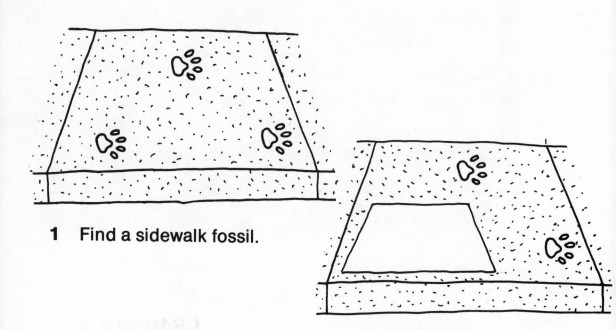

1 Find a sidewalk fossil.

2 Put a piece
of paper over
the fossil.

Rubbings are made by using
a soft sheet of paper, and
a pencil or rubbing crayon.
Rice paper or newsprint
works well.

These soft papers will pick up
the fine lines of a fossil
when a pencil is
rubbed over it.

3 Using a pencil
or crayon go back
and forth across
the fossil.

4 The rubbing
is finished
when the fossil
shows up clearly.

Here are some rubbings of street fossils.

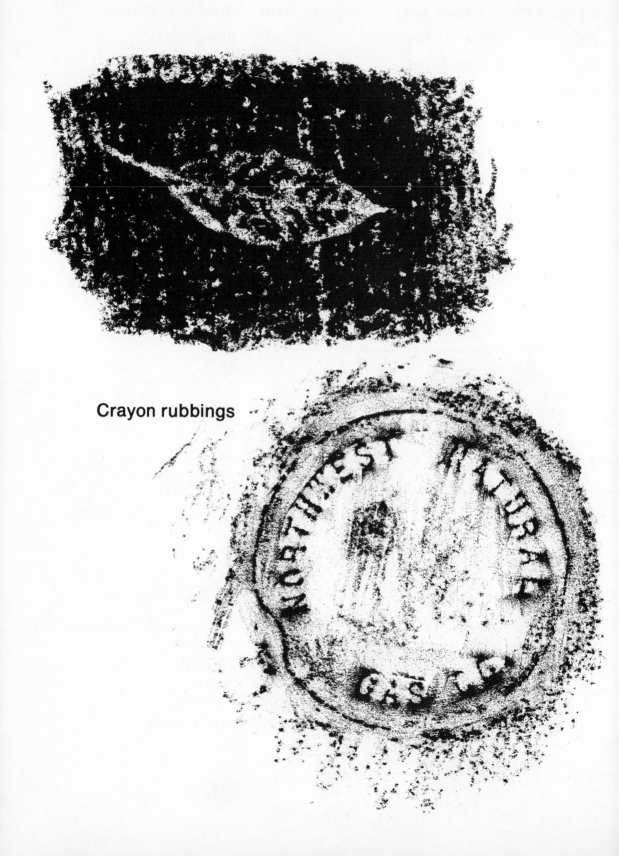

Crayon rubbings

Pencil rubbings

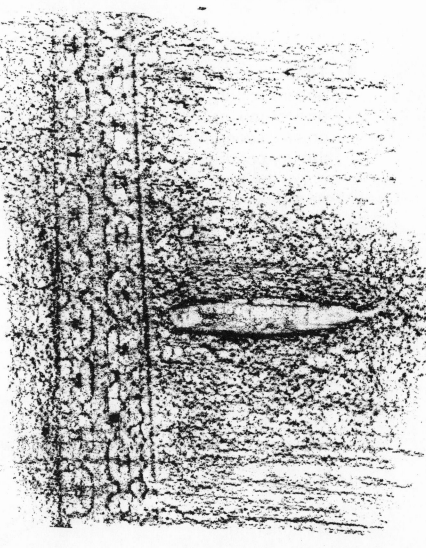

If you want to make your own sidewalk fossils, here's how to do it.

It's fun to hunt for fossils, but if you want to make your own fossils do not use the public sidewalks as some people did in this book. Instead, follow these directions.

Equipment you will need:

1   A bag of dry mixed concrete. All you need to add is water.

2   Three cans:
one for water,
one for mixing,
one for scooping
the dry concrete
out of the bag.
And a stick for mixing.

3   A shallow cardboard box,
or use a large box
cut in half.

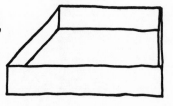

4   A straight piece of wood
or cardboard
or a ruler
to level
the concrete.

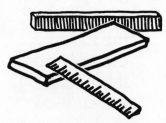

To begin:

5 Pour dry concrete into the can. Slowly add water until the concrete is as thick as oatmeal.

6 Next pour the wet concrete into the box. Make a layer one inch deep.

7 Hold the ruler on its edge. Pull it along the top of the concrete. It will level out the surface.

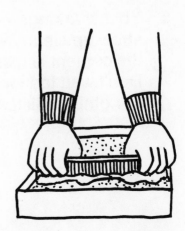

8 Now wait for the concrete to set.
After about 10 minutes
write or draw in the concrete.
If the writing or drawing
does not show up well,
the concrete is still too wet.
Level out the concrete again.
Wait another 10 minutes.
Try again.

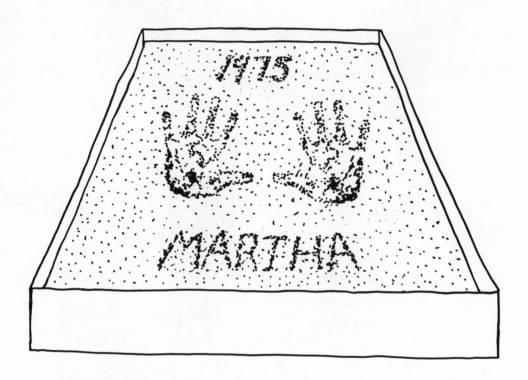

9 Your markings will
show up clearly when
the cement is just dry enough.
Don't wait too long
or nothing will leave a mark.

The sidewalk fossils in this book are from all over the
United States. Now you are ready to look for fossils in
your neighborhood. See if they are very different from the
ones we have found.

What kinds of trees grow on your street?
Do many people have pets?
What kinds of people live there or once lived there?
When was the oldest sidewalk made?

You can learn a lot about your neighborhood by acting as
a sidewalk fossil detective.

ABOUT THE AUTHORS

DR. ROBERT SOMMER is a professor of Psychology and Environmental Studies at the University of California at Davis. His adult books include *Street Art, Design Awareness*, and *Tight Spaces*. He is also a frequent contributor to *Natural History* magazine.

HARRIET BECKER graduated from the University of California at Davis with a B.A. in psychology. She is interested in ceramics, photography, drawing, and oil painting. This is her first children's book.